Pass the LMSW Exam

Pass the LMSW Exam

A Practice Test for the ASWB Master's Level Social Work Licensing Examination

Jeremy Schwartz

Seeley Street Press

Published in the United States of America by:
Seeley Street Press
Salt Lake City, Utah 84103

First Printing, 2022

ISBN: 979-8-9865570-0-7
e-book ISBN: 979-8-9865570-1-4

Publisher's Cataloging-in-Publication Data:
Names: Schwartz, Jeremy, author.
Title: Pass the LMSW Exam : a practice test for the ASWB master's level social work licensing examination / Jeremy Schwartz, LCSW
Description: 2022-2023 Edition. | Salt Lake City, UT : Seeley Street Press, [2022]
Identifiers: LCCN Pending | ISBN 9798986557007
Subjects: LCSH: Social workers – Certification – United States. | Social service – United States – Examinations – Study guides. | Social service – United States – Examinations, questions, etc.
Classification: LOC: HV40.52.A74 2022 | DDC: 361.3076—dc23

CONTENTS

Introduction

Congratulations on taking this important step in your career! As a helping professional, you've worked hard in your graduate social work program, completed your field placements, and now you are preparing to become a licensed professional in your state or province.

Earning your LMSW, however, requires more than knowing the material. The Association of Social Work Boards examination is the test used across the United States and Canada, and it is not easy! However, with advance preparation and expert guidance, you can earn your passing score and become a licensed social worker.

How to Use This Guide

We all lead busy lives, so this guide is designed to avoid wasting your time and get right to what you need. This book is fast-paced so you can go through it multiple times.

First, read through the test taking strategies and content outline. Then, set aside a four-hour block of time to take the practice test.

Once you have taken the practice test, use the quick scoring sheet to mark the questions you got wrong and calculate your score.

Then, take a break because you deserve it! Come back another day to review explanations for the questions you got incorrect. Make sure you fully understand the material.

After that, set aside time to retake the exam. Do this a few times if you need to, until you can correctly answer every question.

Test Format

The Association of Social Work Boards Master's Level exam contains 170 multiple-choice questions. However, as 20 of these questions are experimental, unscored questions being evaluated for future exams, only 150 of the questions will count toward your score. Since the 20 experimental questions are randomly mixed into the exam, you will not know which questions count and which do not. You will have four hours to complete the exam, which is administered by computer at a Pearson VUE testing center.

The Master's Level exam is intended for social workers who have completed their MSW degree but may not yet have post-degree supervision or experience. The test covers material that will hopefully be familiar to you from your MSW graduate program.

The Association of Social Work Boards provides content outlines describing the knowledge, skills, and abilities (KSAs) that the exam is intended to evaluate. Based on these outlines, we know that the exam covers these areas:

- Human development, diversity, and behavior in the environment (27%)
- Assessment and intervention planning (24%)
- Interventions with clients and client systems (24%)
- Professional relationships, values, and ethics (25%)

Three Types of Test Questions

Recall questions

These are the simplest of the question types you will see on the ASWB exams, but they do require knowledge of a wide range of material.

Reasoning questions

Reasoning questions test your ability to consider information from a potential practice scenario and discern a way in which the information connects to a social work theory or practice method.

Application questions

Application questions ask you to put yourself in the shoes of a hypothetical social worker. Using your diverse skillset, you have to apply social work theories or methods to the situation that the question presents.

Study Tips

In your MSW program, you have already learned much of the content that you will need to know for this exam. At the same time, it may have been a long time since you have taken any type of multiple-choice test, let alone a formal, computer-based, standardized exam. Here are some tips to make sure you make the most of your preparation:

1. Study for four hours at a time.
Being a social worker in the field can at times feel like a test of endurance, and this exam is no different. Four hours is a long time to sit at the testing center and take your exam. Fatigue is normal, but with practice you can build up your ability to focus over long periods of time. Work some endurance training into your exam prep by setting aside four hour blocks to study without distractions or interruptions.

2. Practice, practice, practice.
The more practice questions you review ahead of time, the more familiar you will be with the exam format and the types of questions you will encounter. Take the time to go through the practice questions in this book and make sure you understand how to apply your knowledge and skills to the different types of exam questions.

3. Know the basics.
As a social worker, you may work in a particular field of practice and as a result you have specialized knowledge in this area. This specialized

knowledge will be helpful when you take your licensing exam. At the same time, it is important to come to the exam with a wide enough knowledge base to be able to answer questions about a range of practice areas. Make sure you know the material that every social worker needs to know, in addition to some specialized knowledge here and there. The exam requires knowing "a little bit about a lot," so make sure your preparation scratches the surface of many areas of social work theories, models, and perspectives.

Testing Accommodations

The ASWB offers a variety of accommodations, which they refer to as nonstandard testing arrangements, for exam candidates who qualify. Accommodations are available for candidates with documented disabilities or health conditions, including pregnancy and lactation needs. Depending on the policies of the state or provincial social work board, accommodations may also be available for candidates who use English as a second language.

I have encountered many students who are excellent social workers but who have had difficulty with this exam due to attention and learning disabilities. If you may benefit from accommodations, do not hesitate to apply for them.

To apply for nonstandard testing arrangements, you can fill out the form that is posted on the ASWB website. Make sure to do this before registering for your exam.

Test-Taking Tips

In your social work program, you were likely evaluated based on written papers, process recordings, and clinical supervision, with very few written exams. At this point in your career, multiple-choice tests may seem like a distant memory. Because of this, it is important to review some test-taking tips so you can succeed on the exam. Here are my top recommendations:

1. Pace yourself.

Four hours is a long time, so do not rush. Make sure to read each question carefully, as well as all of the answer choices, so that you can choose the *best* answer. On the other hand, if you find you are getting stuck on a question, flag it for later and move on to the next question.

2. Trust your instincts.

Once you have selected the best answer choice, don't second-guess it! Students sometimes are hesitant to go with an answer that seems "too easy," but some of the questions really are just checking that you know the literal definition of a word. If you know the answer, take credit for what you know!

3. Identify the knowledge and skills being tested.

Each question is testing your knowledge, skills, or abilities about a particular social work theory, model, or intervention. For example, questions about social work ethics will require applying content from the NASW Code of Ethics (rather than your opinion about what is ethical) to the case vignette. By identifying what the question is testing you on, you can make sure to answer based on your textbook knowledge rather than based on personal instinct.

4. Pay close attention to key test question terms such as "most," "first," "next," "best," "not," and "except."

Exam questions will sometimes include a signal word at or near the end of the question stem. On these questions, you may encounter multiple answer choices that seem to reflect good social work practice. However, only one of the answers will best fit the question stem given the signal word presented.

5. Take breaks when you need them.

It's a marathon, not a sprint, and it's important you are focused as you answer each question. You may get fatigued after some time, so don't hesitate to get up, go to the restroom, and stretch your legs. While the breaks do count toward your test time, you should still have plenty of time when you return.

6. Use the test software to your advantage.

The new format of the test software allows you to highlight and cross out words. You won't need to do this for every question, but make sure to use these tools for those tougher questions where you see a signal word like "most" or "next," or when you need to use process of elimination.

7. Remember to breathe, and don't worry.

It's normal to have test anxiety, so practice self care as you go. Remember, only good things can come from this exam, and you can always retake it on that small chance that you don't pass the first time.

Developing Your Study Schedule

You've taken a significant step in your career by registering for the LMSW exam. It will take a good amount of work, but you can do it! Break down your studying according to the amount of time you have between now and your test date. You've got this!

It is important to review social work content as well as practice exam questions. Take a few moments to write down your plan using the prompts below.

Week 1

Content review:

_____

_____

_____

_____

Practice question review:

_____

_____

_____

_____

Week 2

Content review:

_____

_____

_____

_____

Practice question review:

_____

_____

_____

_____

Week 3

Content review:

_____

_____

_____

_____

Practice question review:

_____

_____

_____

_____

Week 4

Content review:

_____

_____

_____

_____

Practice question review:

_____

_____

_____

_____

150-Question Practice Test

To help you prepare, I've included a 150-question practice exam here. Since only 150 questions out of the 170 on the ASWB exam are scored, your performance on these 150 questions will give you a sense of where you currently stand. Set aside some time to complete the entire test, if possible. When you have finished, you can check your answers and review the explanations to any questions you may have had difficulty with.

1. Erickson's psychosocial stage of ego integrity versus despair refers to which of the following periods in the human lifespan?

    A. Early childhood
    B. Late adolescence
    C. Middle adulthood
    D. Older adulthood

2. Which of the following is NOT a true statement about spiritual development throughout the life course?

    A. There are multiple models that attempt to explain the impact of religious and spiritual beliefs on human behavior.
    B. Models of spiritual development tend to move from an egocentric state, to a conformist state, to a universalist or integrative state.

C. Spirituality may help individuals to cope with events that are out of their control.

D. There is a negative relationship between spirituality and mental health.

3. A client reports that he had committed to walking a friend's dog the day before but did not do so because he was tired. The client felt guilty about not walking the dog, and tried to make himself feel better by making a donation to a local animal shelter. The client is most likely using which of the following psychological defense mechanisms?

A. Conversion
B. Repression
C. Regression
D. Undoing

4. A social worker is meeting with a heterosexual couple that reports having had numerous recent disagreements. The husband is upset that his wife does not cook dinner every night, and the wife is upset that her husband is making less money than she is. The social worker asks the husband and wife how they each view their roles in terms of gender, and asks them to consider if they might want their roles in the relationship to look different. The social worker is most likely applying principles of:

A. Feminist theory
B. Social learning theory
C. Classical conditioning
D. Operant conditioning

5. A social worker meets with a client and completes a biopsychosocial assessment. The use of the biopsychosocial assessment is most consistent with which of the following theories?

A. Person-in-environment theory
B. Empowerment theory
C. Feminist theory
D. Freudian theory

6. After a therapy group has been meeting for several weeks, group members begin to experience conflict with one another and appear to compete to have their ideas heard. The group is MOST LIKELY in which stage of group development?

A. Norming
B. Forming
C. Storming
D. Performing

7. Which of the following is the BEST description of the purpose of crisis intervention?

A. To assist an individual affected by a crisis to stabilize and to reduce potential harm
B. A model of psychotherapy for individuals who frequently experience crisis
C. A secondary prevention technique for individuals at risk of crisis
D. An approach that can be short-term or long-term, depending on available resources

8. Resilience theory includes all of the following principles EXCEPT:

A. Clients can survive and thrive even when facing difficult circumstances.
B. People have the ability to grow and adapt.
C. People can mobilize internal and external resources to improve a situation.

D. Social problems are a result of underlying psychopathology.

9. According to the DSM-5, which of the following statements is true about persistent complex bereavement disorder?

A. The disorder is only diagnosed if at least 12 months have passed (in adults), or 6 months have passed (in children), since the death of someone close to the bereaved person.
B. The disorder is only diagnosed if at least 2 weeks have passed (in adults), or 4 weeks have passed (in children), since the death of someone close to the bereaved person.
C. The disorder is only diagnosed in specific social and cultural groups
D. The disorder is only diagnosed in clients who also have a co-occurring disorder such as major depressive disorder

10. Which of the following is NOT a component of psychodynamic theory?

A. The unconscious mind has an influence on personality
B. Childhood experiences have an influence on personality
C. People use defense mechanisms to protect against overwhelming or uncomfortable feelings
D. Human behavior is impacted by conditioning and reinforcement

11. A child meets with a school social worker, who notices a cast on his arm. The child states that he had to go to the hospital after his father threw him down the stairs, but that it was his fault because he misbehaved. He states he will make sure it will not happen again, and that there is nothing to worry about. What should the social worker do FIRST?

A. Ask a supervisor if the incident should be reported

B. Report the incident to the state's mandated reporter hotline

C. Schedule an appointment with the parents to find out more about what happened

D. Check with the hospital where the child received the cast to find out how severe the injury was

12. Gender identity is different from gender expression in which of the following ways?

A. Gender identity refers to a person's felt sense of being male, female, or another gender, while gender expression refers to a person's outward appearance and behaviors associated with masculinity and femininity.

B. Gender identity is scientifically based, while gender expression is socially constructed

C. Gender expression is scientifically based, while gender identity is socially constructed

D. Gender identity refers to a person's official documents, while gender expression refers to a person's LGBTQ experience

13. Which of the following statements is NOT true about bisexual identity?

A. Bisexuality is a temporary phase until an individual determines their orientation as gay or heterosexual

B. Bisexuality is defined as the experience of being attracted to individuals of more than one gender

C. Bisexuality includes romantic attraction, sexual attraction, and sexual behavior

D. Bisexual people experience discrimination from both outside and within the LGBTQ community

14. Social justice is BEST defined as:

A. The belief that every person deserves equal rights and opportunities

B. The idea that everyone should have equal economic resources

C. A principle that guides macro social work practice

D. A component of critical race theory

15. A social worker assists a group of activists to plan a community town hall on the topic of climate change in order to mobilize support for local legislation that would implement policies to help the city prepare for natural disasters and other environmental impacts of climate change. The social worker is most likely to use which of the following theories or models in this work?

A. Person-in-environment

B. Community organizing

C. Classical conditioning

D. Social learning

16. A mental status examination includes all of the following components EXCEPT:

A. Appearance

B. Mood

C. Thought process

D. Diagnosis

17. After terminating treatment, a client requests a copy of his records and completes a signed authorization for the records to be mailed to him. The social worker reviews the chart and confirms that there is no information in the records that is likely to be harmful to the client. The social worker should NEXT:

A. Inform the client that records requests must be completed in person so that the social worker can assist the client in interpreting the information they contain.

B. Send the records to the client, and offer to meet with the client if he would like assistance in interpreting them.

C. Inform the client that a valid reason for the request must be provided before the social worker can proceed

D. Invoke client-therapist privilege and ask a judge to invalidate the request for records.

18. A social worker is conducting practice evaluation research and decides to conduct baseline measures of client progress at the start of treatment. Clients will then complete symptom questionnaires once during a course of short term therapy, and then complete one set of post-intervention measurement scales. Which type of research design best represents the social worker's practice evaluation?

A. ABA
B. ABAB
C. ABC
D. AB

19. Which of the following is an evidence-based treatment for emotion dysregulation associated with borderline personality disorder?

A. Imago therapy
B. The Gottman method
C. Dialectical behavior therapy
D. Psychoanalytic psychotherapy

20. All of the following are true statements about cultural competence EXCEPT:

A. The *NASW Code of Ethics* includes standards on cultural competence and diversity
B. Cultural competence requires a flexible and individualized approach
C. Social workers should support policies that respect difference and human rights
D. Social workers should only treat clients with the same cultural background as their own.

21. Harm reduction is BEST defined as:

A. Policies and interventions intended to minimize the adverse consequences of substance abuse without requiring the client to stop using
B. A 12-step model of peer support
C. An abstinence based model of substance use treatment
D. A model focused on relapse prevention

22. A client is meeting with a social worker and describing his reasons for seeking help. The social worker listens closely, avoids interrupting, and reflects back what he has heard the client say. The social worker is most likely using which of the following techniques?

A. Ericksonian hypnoisis
B. Active listening
C. Social diagnosis
D. Anger management

23. All of the following are clinical benefits of role play techniques EXCEPT:

A. Role play can improve interpersonal skills
B. Role play can improve communication

C. Role play can teach empathy

D. Role play can require preparation and explanation

24. A client is court mandated to therapy following a recent incident of violence. The social worker teaches the client skills for relaxation such as deep breathing, as well as how to put situations into a larger perspective and how to walk away from situations that are likely to get him upset. The social worker is most likely using techniques of:

A. Anger management

B. Psychoanalysis

C. Interpersonal psychotherapy

D. Motivational interviewing

25. After a meeting of a facilitated support group, a client approaches the social worker and states that she has been having difficulty opening up in the group. She feels like she is the only one going through the stressors that she has been facing, and she is not sure that anyone else will understand. The social worker should:

A. Schedule an appointment to meet with the client for individual therapy

B. Refer the client to a psychiatrist for a medication evaluation

C. Encourage the client to bring this issue up at the next group session

D. Find a different group for the client to attend

26. Which of the following is a true statement about social workers' ethical responsibilities with regard to social justice issues?

A. Social workers must remain neutral on controversial issues.

B. Social workers have a responsibility to engage in social and political action.

C. Social workers should focus exclusively on clinical practice.

D. Social workers should engage primarily in macro practice.

27. According to Freud, the anal stage of psychosexual development refers to:

A. A stage that takes place approximately between the ages of 18 months to three years, in which pleasure is derived from controlling bladder and bowel movement

B. A stage in which adults become overly controlling or easily angered

C. A stage in which sexuality is latent

D. A stage that begins after puberty

28. A needs assessment refers to:

A. A method of social work education

B. A social program for high-need groups

C. A process for evaluating insufficiencies and gaps in services

D. A method of clinical supervision

29. According to the professional value of competence, social workers should:

A. Report any colleagues who appear to be incompetent

B. Engage in regular competency testing

C. Practice in areas for which they are qualified, and strive to increase their knowledge

D. Not begin working with clients until they have completed their professional education

30. According to the NASW Code of Ethics, all of the following are core values of the social work profession except:

A. Service

B. Voting

C. Integrity

D. Social justice

31. Networking in social work practice involves all of the following EXCEPT:

A. Sharing of resources and expertise

B. Identifying candidates for job openings

C. Establishing professional relationships with other clinicians

D. Exchanging business opportunities with clients

32. Quality assurance processes in social work do NOT involve:

A. Incorporation of quality assurance standards throughout an agency

B. Gathering data and information on outcomes

C. Use of data analysis to make improvements

D. Placing a hiring freeze to avoid budget deficits

33. Cost effectiveness refers MOST specifically to:

A. A type of program evaluation that looks at the financial efficiency with which a program produces specific nonmonetary benefits

B. A determination of whether the costs of a program exceed its benefits

C. An evaluation of whether a program is achieving its goals

D. The use of programmatic changes to improve outcomes

34. A social work colleague confides in you that she drank two beers in the morning before coming to work. According to the *NASW Code of Ethics*, you should FIRST:

A. Report the incident to your state licensing board

B. Discuss the situation with your supervisor

C. Call 911 so she can be taken to the emergency room for a psychiatric evaluation

D. Discuss your concerns with the colleague and assist her in making a plan to address her drinking

35. All of the following are functions of an institutional review board except:

A. Protecting the rights and welfare of human subjects in medical and behavioral research

B. Approving and monitoring research activities within its jurisdiction

C. Reviewing course evaluations to assess social work educators' effectiveness in teaching

D. Determining the adequacy of measures to protect the privacy of human subjects and the confidentiality of data

36. In conducting research on young children, the researcher should:

A. Obtain informed consent of the parent or guardian and verbal assent from the child participants

B. Obtain informed consent of both the parent or guardian and the child

C. Obtain assent of both the parent or guardian and the child

D. Obtain verbal assent from the parent or guardian and informed consent from the child

37. All of the following are models of supervision and consultation EXCEPT:

A. Individual

B. Family

C. Group

D. Peer

38. A client requests a social worker's assistance in changing his sexual orientation from gay to straight. The social worker should:

A. Inform the client that such practices have been discredited and found to be harmful, and offer to discuss the client's feelings about being gay
B. Refer the client to a colleague who provides these services
C. Ask the client if he has religious beliefs that prohibit homosexuality
D. Refer the client for spiritual counseling

39. According to Maslow's hierarchy, the most basic level of needs consists of:

A. Safety needs
B. Belonging and love needs
C. Physiological needs
D. Esteem needs

40. A 51-year-old client recently lost his mother, who died suddenly. The client reports feeling confused, stating, "There must have been some misunderstanding. It can't have been her. I just saw her last week." The client is most likely experiencing which of Kubler-Ross' stages of grief?

A. Anger
B. Acceptance
C. Depression
D. Denial

41. Which of the following is the correct order of steps in the problem-solving process?

A. Engagement, assessment, termination, evaluation, planning, intervention

B. Engagement, assessment, planning, intervention, evaluation, termination

C. Assessment, engagement, planning, intervention, evaluation, termination

D. Assessment, planning, engagement, intervention, evaluation, termination

42. A parent reports being concerned about her 4-year old child who has been talking about an imaginary friend. The social worker should FIRST:

A. Conduct a comprehensive biopsychosocial-cultural-spiritual assessment of the child

B. Interview the child to assess the child's capacity for reality testing

C. Reassure the parent that having imaginary friends is normal, as pretend play is a part of Piaget's preoperational stage of development

D. Explore the parent's feelings about the distinction between reality and fantasy

43. Professional development consists of all of the following EXCEPT:

A. Reviewing published literature

B. Attending in-service trainings

C. Participating in workshops related to social work practice

D. Conducting intake assessments

44. In order to maintain the confidentiality of client information, social workers should do which of the following:

A. When information must be disclosed, disclose only the minimum amount of confidential information necessary to achieve the purpose of the disclosure

B. Avoid discussing confidential information in public or semi-public areas

C. Ensure that clients' records are stored in a secure location

D. All of the above

45. Transference is different from countertransference in that:

A. Transference refers to a client's feelings that are redirected toward the therapist, while countertransference refers to a therapist's feelings that are redirected toward a client

B. Transference refers to a therapist's feelings that are redirected toward a client, while countertransference refers to a client's feelings that are redirected toward the therapist

C. Transference refers to the practice of referring clients out to other agencies, while countertransference refers to intake of clients transferred from other agencies

D. Transference refers to intake of clients referred from other agencies, while countertransference refers to the practice of referring clients out to other agencies

46. Which of the following is NOT true regarding time management?

A. Time management aims to increase effectiveness and productivity.

B. Time management is used in both business and personal applications.

C. Time management is best implemented by addressing only urgent issues and devoting most time to "putting out fires."

D. Time management involves categorizing activities based on importance and urgency.

47. Compassion fatigue is BEST defined as:

A. Being tired after a long day at the office as a compassionate social worker

B. Emotional and physical exhaustion that inhibits one's capacity to empathize or feel compassion for others

C. An ego defense mechanism

D. Professional burnout

48. Social transitions typically associated with late adulthood include all of the following EXCEPT:

A. Retirement
B. Widowhood
C. Grandparenthood
D. Eco-mapping

49. According to the life course perspective, the concept of linked lives is most closely associated with:

A. Infancy and early childhood
B. Adolescence
C. Middle adulthood
D. Late adulthood

50. Cognitive development that involves an increasing capacity for foresight and abstract thinking occurs during:

A. Adolescence and early adulthood
B. Middle adulthood
C. Late adulthood
D. Infancy

51. Key social transitions associated with development from adolescence into early adulthood include:

A. Employment
B. Relationship formation
C. Independent living
D. All of the above

52. A family meets with a social worker for therapy. They state that their son frequently gets into arguments with them and does not do as he is told. They ask the social worker to "fix" their son so that he can better get along with family members. Other family members do not identify any problems with their own behavior or with family dynamics. The family's identification of the son as the patient for the social worker to "fix" is mostly a result of which process?

A. Child development
B. Scapegoating
C. Cognitive development
D. Classical conditioning

53. Sexual paraphilias can be BEST understood through the lens of:

A. Classical conditioning
B. Social learning theory
C. Empowerment theory
D. Systems theory

54. The work of John Bowlby is associated with:

A. Attachment theory
B. Social learning theory
C. Systems theory
D. Behaviorism

55. Attachment is best defined as:

A. A strong emotional bond that an infant forms with their caregiver, as well as the process by which the infant forms this bond
B. The connection between micro, mezzo, and macro systems in social work practice
C. The role of a researcher using the participant-observation method
D. The second of Erickson's stages of psychosocial development

56. According to the work of Abraham Maslow, basic needs include:

  A. Self-actualization
  B. Generativity vs. stagnation
  C. Inferiority vs. shame and doubt
  D. Physiological needs

57. Adult children caring for aging parents are most likely to experience:

  A. Psychological stress associated with caregiving responsibilities
  B. Narcissistic injury
  C. Projective identification
  D. Secondary trauma

58. A client meets with a social worker for the first time. At the beginning of the session, the client informs the social worker that the client uses they/them pronouns. To best support the client's dignity and right to self-determination, the social worker should:

  A. Conduct a focused biopsychosocial assessment with an emphasis on the client's gender identity
  B. Thank the client for sharing their pronouns and use they/them pronouns when referring to the client
  C. Ask the client how long they have used these pronouns
  D. Ignore this information as it is not the focus of the session

59. The life review approach to resolving and integrating past conflicts is most closely associated with:

  A. Psychosexual development
  B. The concrete operational stage
  C. Narrative gerontology
  D. Quantitative research

60. Healthy defenses differ from neurotic defenses in that:

A. Healthy defenses conserve energy for daily life responsibilities, while neurotic defenses limit the user's ability to manage everyday life and relationships.

B. Healthy defenses refer to those used by the social worker, while neurotic defenses refer to those use by the client.

C. Healthy defenses are a sign of ego strength while neurotic defenses are a sign of ego weakness.

D. Healthy defenses refer to those used by medical professionals, while neurotic defenses refer to those used by mental health professionals.

61. Parentification refers to:

A. A life transition in which an individual becomes a parent for the first time

B. A role reversal in which a child takes on emotional and practical responsibilities for their parents or other family members

C. A coming-of-age experience in which a young adult becomes ready for parenthood

D. An ego defense mechanism common in new parents

62. An 18-year-old client meets with a social worker and informs the social worker that she is transgender and plans to obtain medical services as part of her transition from male to female. The client requests a letter from the social worker attesting to her gender identity. She informs the social worker that her doctor requires this letter. To best serve this client, the social worker should:

A. Assess the client for possible gender dysphoria and any mental health conditions, and provide a referral letter if appropriate

B. Refer the client to a social worker who identifies as LGBTQ

C. Discuss the case with the client's parents

D. Request a copy of the client's medical records

63. All of the following are signs of burnout EXCEPT:

    A. Physical exhaustion
    B. Feeling ineffective in one's work
    C. Increased irritability
    D. Scheduling of vacation and personal time

64. Person-in-environment theory is BEST defined as:

    A. A psychosocial perspective that understands people's experience in terms of how they interact with, and act upon, the systems in their lives
    B. A psychodynamic perspective that looks at children's early experiences with their caregivers as impacting later development
    C. A Jungian perspective that understands people's experiences in terms of their unconscious shadow archetypes
    D. A social policy perspective that involves conducting needs assessments for various populations

65. Which of the following is a true statement regarding burnout?

    A. Burnout is clear evidence that a social worker has not prioritized self-care.
    B. It is very common to experience burnout in social work.
    C. Burnout is always the fault of the individual.
    D. Resilient social workers do not experience burnout.

66. According to the eco-structural model of therapy:

    A. Psychotherapy techniques must be rooted in an awareness of ecological issues.
    B. Families seeking help must be connected to other families in similar situations, in order to provide mutual support and an increased sense of community.
    C. Ecological structures form the basis for determining interventions.

D. Psychopathology can be understood through an exploration of childhood conflicts.

67. A social worker receives a subpoena from an attorney requesting treatment records for a former client. The social worker should:

A. Object to the subpoena
B. Release the records requested
C. Ignore the subpoena
D. Redact information from the records

68. Based on the Tarasoff decision:

A. Mental health professionals have a duty to warn and protect individuals who are threatened with physical harm by a client.
B. Client information is entirely confidential and can never be released without client consent.
C. Social workers should break confidentiality when a client is at risk of suicide.
D. Clients can be admitted to a hospital involuntarily when they pose a danger to themselves or others.

69. Confidentiality of client information must be preserved:

A. For the duration of the social worker - client relationship
B. For 5 years following termination
C. For 3 years following termination
D. Indefinitely, even after a client is deceased

70. An ethical dilemma refers to:

A. A situation in which a social worker is unknowingly acting in an unethical manner
B. A situation in which following one ethical principle appears to require going against a different ethical principle

C. A situation in which a social worker is knowingly acting in an unethical manner

D. A legal determination of unethical behavior

71. A school social worker is working with a student who had recently instigated a physical altercation with another student. The social worker plans a circle for the affected parties to gather and listen to one another, and to develop a plan to repair the harm that was done. The social worker is most likely applying the principles of:

A. Distributive justice
B. Social justice
C. Economic justice
D. Restorative justice

72. To address the impacts of structural racism, social workers should:

A. Engage in social and political action
B. Attend cultural competency trainings
C. Discuss countertransference in supervision
D. Maintain neutrality and objectivity

73. A client discloses that he is feeling attracted toward his social worker. The social worker should:

A. Terminate services immediately
B. Refer the client to a social worker of a different gender
C. Tell the client that these feelings are inappropriate
D. Explore the client's feelings while maintaining appropriate boundaries

74. Assertiveness training is NOT used to help clients:

A. Deal with frustrating situations
B. Make requests

C. Refuse requests

D. Engage in unhelpful conflict

75. Which of the following is a true statement regarding the relationship between social policy and social work practice?

A. Social work practitioners should remain neutral on issues of social policy.

B. Social policy determines, to a significant extent, the way that social work is practiced.

C. Social policy and social work practice are entirely separate fields

D. Social policy and social work practice are only slightly related

76. Active listening involves all of the following EXCEPT:

A. Asking open-ended questions

B. Paying attention to body language

C. Reflecting back what is heard

D. Interrupting

77. A social worker has been newly hired for an administrative role and one of his responsibilities is staff training. To best meet the needs of staff, the social worker should FIRST:

A. Conduct a staff training needs assessment

B. Organize as many trainings as possible

C. Postpone staff training as it is not a core administrative function

D. Schedule at least one training per month

78. An empirically based approach to social work research refers to:

A. Research based on observed and measured experiences

B. Research funded by nation-states or empires

C. Qualitative research only

D. Quantitative research only

79. In accordance with a task-centered model:

A. Behavioral approaches are used to promote completion of a task to produce measurable outcomes
B. Social workers should complete as many tasks as possible during the work day
C. Psychoanalytic diagnosis is used to understand personality structure
D. Clinical supervision is a requirement for all social workers

80. Evidence-based practice is BEST defined as:

A. The use of research and data to guide policy and practice decisions
B. The use of manualized treatments to ensure consistent practice
C. The exclusive use of cognitive behavioral therapy with all clients
D. The exclusive use of psychodynamic psychotherapy with all clients

81. Qualitative research is different than quantitative research in that:

A. Qualitative research is of a higher quality than quantitative research
B. Qualitative research involves empirical methods, while quantitative research does not involve empirical methods
C. Qualitative research does not involve empirical methods, while quantitative research involves empirical methods
D. Qualitative research involves the collection of non-numerical data, while quantitative research involves the collection of numerical data

82. One benefit of using qualitative research methods is that they:

A. Utilize deductive rather than inductive reasoning
B. Are more accurate than quantitative research methods
C. Ensure a high quality of results

D. Can shift research questions from those of the researcher to those that are central to the participants

83. Single-subject design refers to:

   A. A method of research in which the participant serves as their own control
   B. A randomized controlled trial
   C. Participant-observer research
   D. Research conducted using exclusively qualitative methods

84. According to structural family therapy:

   A. The therapist should strive to "join" the family system in order to understand its unwritten rules
   B. Pathology is a result of individuals' deficits
   C. Problems in the family system are the result of individuals' fixations in the oral and anal stages
   D. Family problems are the result of reinforcement and punishment

85. Executive functioning is BEST defined as:

   A. A style of management in which high-level executives are responsibility for the majority of organizational functions
   B. A set of cognitive processes and skills that help an individual plan for and carry out their goals
   C. A system of mental deficits that cause psychiatric disorders
   D. The mental status of a person with attention-deficit/hyperactivity disorder

86. In dialectical behavior therapy, mindfulness skills are used to:

   A. Improve emotion regulation and decrease rumination
   B. Promote a task-centered model

C. Conduct motivational interviewing

D. Assess readiness to change

87. Which of the following is NOT a phase in standard models of trauma-informed care?

A. Safety and stabilization

B. Mourning and remembrance

C. Avoidance and re-experiencing

D. Reconnection and reintegration

88. Which of the following is NOT true regarding self-disclosure?

A. Self-disclosure is always unethical in social work practice

B. Some self-disclosure can be beneficial in therapy

C. Self-disclosure can at times be harmful to clients

D. Self-disclosure can potentially indicate a boundary violation

89. Types of advocacy include all of the following EXCEPT:

A. Self advocacy

B. Case advocacy

C. Class advocacy

D. Privilege advocacy

90. A 17-year-old male is referred to a social worker after his parents become concerned that he is not eating enough. The client reports that he restricts his eating because is afraid of gaining weight and that he wants to make sure he does not become obese. He worries that he is already overweight, even though his weight and height are reflective of a low body-mass index. What is the client's most likely DSM-5 diagnosis?

A. Anorexia nervosa

B. Bulimia nervosa

C. Avoidant/restrictive food intake disorder (ARFID)

D. Rumination disorder

91. A 35 year old male meets with a social worker and describes feeling very badly about himself. He was recently fired from his job due to poor performance. He reports seeing himself as lazy and believing that he is a failure. According to the principles of person-centered therapy, the social worker can best help the client by:

A. Providing empathy and unconditional positive regard
B. Exploring the origin of the client's negative beliefs
C. Challenging the client's irrational beliefs
D. Helping the client find solutions so he can be more successful in his next job

92. When communicating with clients by email, social workers should NOT:

A. Send confidential client information in unencrypted messages
B. Take steps to protect the confidentiality of electronic communications
C. Develop policies and procedures for notifying clients of any breach of confidential information
D. Avoid sending messages for non-work-related purposes

93. A 25 year old male meets with a social worker. The client reports that for the past week he has felt especially energetic, has not felt much of a need to sleep, and has been very talkative. He reports being especially productive in his work during this time, even as he has been spending large amounts of money, which he cannot afford, and has been engaging in high-risk sexual behavior. The client states he has a history of depressive episodes as well. What is the client's most likely DSM-5 diagnosis?

A. Bipolar I disorder
B. Bipolar II disorder

C. Major depressive disorder, recurrent, moderate

D. None of the above

94. A 40 year old female meets with a social worker for help reducing negative thoughts that she has about herself. The social worker instructs the client to accept her emotions rather than try to deny them, to reflect on her personal values, and to plan concrete steps that she can take to live according to her values. The social worker is most likely using techniques of:

A. Cognitive behavioral therapy

B. Psychodynamic psychotherapy

C. Acceptance and commitment therapy

D. Interpersonal psychotherapy

95. A social worker conducts an initial session with a 25 year old female client. The client was recently discharged from a psychiatric inpatient unit after a suicide attempt. The client reports feeling empty, experiencing intense fears of abandonment, and engaging in self-harm behaviors. To best assist this client, the social worker should develop a treatment plan that will most likely include:

A. Cognitive behavioral therapy

B. Neuro-linguistic programming

C. Dialectical behavior therapy

D. Single session consultation

96. Forensic social work refers to:

A. The regular use of fingerprinting and background checks as part of the hiring process

B. Social work practice that is related to legal issues or to criminal or civil legal systems

C. A method of social work research

D. Statistical analysis of social work data

97. The difference between empathy and sympathy is that:

   A. Empathy involves understanding or imagining how someone might feel, while sympathy involves sharing the feelings of another person
   B. Sympathy involves understanding or imagining how someone might feel, while empathy involves sharing the feelings of another person
   C. Empathy involves emotions that are explicitly stated while sympathy involves emotions that are not explicitly stated
   D. Sympathy is relevant to social work practice while empathy is only used in non social work contexts

98. The Rorschach test involves the use of:

   A. Multiple choice questions
   B. Essay questions
   C. Inkblots
   D. Medical examinations

99. Which of the following is the correct order of Tuckman's stages of group development?

   A. Forming, storming, norming, performing
   B. Norming, forming, storming, performing
   C. Forming, norming, storming, performing
   D. Norming, storming, forming, performing

100. You have been contracted by an agency to conduct an evaluation in order to determine the effectiveness of their program. What should you do FIRST?

   A. Identify the program's goals
   B. Utilize a process evaluation to understand how services are carried out

C. Define measurable outcomes

D. Utilize qualitative and/or quantitative measures

101. A hospital social worker meets with a female adult patient and notices that the patient has several scars and bruises on her arms. When she asks the patient questions, the patient's partner often interjects and answers for her. To best evaluate this patient's needs, the social worker should:

A. Meet with the partner first for collateral information

B. Ask the partner to step out, and then interview the patient

C. Review the patient's medical records to better assess the situation

D. Obtain collateral information from the multidisciplinary team

102. A social worker at a local family service agency observes a lack of services to meet the needs of the Native American community. To best advocate for the Native American community, the social worker should FIRST:

A. Seek out cultural competency training

B. Assess the specific needs of the Native American community in this area

C. Develop programs of interest to the Native American community

D. Conduct research on Native American health outcomes

103. A social worker has been hired to assist a labor union with community organizing efforts. To best engage with the union community, the social worker should FIRST:

A. Immerse themself into the community to begin to understand community dynamics and build relationships

B. Create goals and objectives for organizing in this community

C. Meet with influential community leaders

D. Develop an action plan

104. According to Carol Gilligan's challenge to Kohlberg's theory of moral development:

A. Women make moral and ethical decisions based on how they will affect others
B. Moral development occurs through the stages of denial, anger, bargaining, depression, and acceptance
C. Moral development cannot be defined using a stage theory
D. Moral development is best explained through Freudian psychology

105. A group of high school students organizes a walk-out to protest against gun violence. One student declines to participate, even though he agrees with the cause, because he thinks it is wrong to walk out of class when the student handbook states that students must remain in each class for the entire class period. The student's thinking most closely resembles which stage of moral development?

A. Egocentrism
B. Pre-conventional morality
C. Conventional morality
D. Post-conventional morality

106. Which of the following statements is consistent with the principles of narrative therapy?

A. Individuals make meaning through the novels and short stories they read.
B. People's behavior is driven by how they interpret their experiences.
C. People's behavior is driven by reinforcement and punishment.
D. Individuals make meaning through conditioned stimuli.

107. A 65-year-old client was recently fired from his job due to failure to complete assigned tasks. He states that it does not matter anyway,

as he had been planning to retire within the next few years and is glad to be done working. The client is MOST likely using the defense mechanism of:

A. Projection
B. Projective identification
C. Rationalization
D. Intellectualization

108. Gender identity is different from biological sex in that:

A. Gender identity refers to a person's felt sense of being male, female, non-binary, or any other gender, while biological sex refers to a person's physical traits associated with being male, female, and/or intersex.
B. Gender identity refers to membership in the LGBTQ community while biological sex refers to being cisgender.
C. Gender identity refers to exclusively male and female identities, while biological sex can be male, female, or intersex.
D. Gender identity refers to physical characteristics while biological sex refers to medical documentation only.

109. A social worker is meeting with a client who was referred for a dialectical behavior therapy skills group. The client reports that no one in her family seems to listen or care about her except when she is suicidal. When the client makes suicidal gestures, her family rallies around her and mobilizes to take care of her. Based on the principles of operant conditioning, the client's behavior has most likely continued as a result of:

A. Positive punishment
B. Negative punishment
C. Positive reinforcement
D. Negative reinforcement

110. A 25-year-old client is referred to a social worker by his primary care physician. The client reports feeling tired, having a lack of appetite, feeling sad every day, and crying often. He states that these symptoms have lasted for the past three weeks. What is the client's MOST likely DSM-5 diagnosis?

A. Major depressive disorder
B. Generalized anxiety disorder
C. Schizophrenia
D. Cannabis use disorder

111. At the hospital unit where you work, you notice that a colleague has been coming to work late, failing to complete documentation, and frequently missing staff meetings. You are concerned about the impact of these behaviors on clients and on your team. What should you do FIRST?

A. Report the colleague's behavior to your supervisor.
B. Speak with the colleague about your concerns.
C. Report the colleague's behavior to the state board.
D. Ask other team members if they have noticed these behaviors.

112. All of the following are true about telemental health EXCEPT:

A. Telemental health services provide certain advantages, particularly with regard to access for clients living in areas with limited mental health services.
B. Telemental health services are exactly the same as in-person services and require no special considerations.
C. Social workers must obtain informed consent when providing telemental health services.
D. Social workers must consider the licensure requirements of the states in which they are licensed as well as the states in which clients are located.

113. All of the following are true about confidentiality EXCEPT:

    A. In group settings, social workers should inform clients that confidentiality cannot be guaranteed.
    B. Social workers must keep client information confidential, with no exceptions.
    C. Social workers should discuss with clients their policies regarding confidentiality and its limits.
    D. There are circumstances in which it is necessary to break confidentiality.

114. A client wishes to obtain an abortion but lives in a state in which abortion access is restricted. In this state, there is no law against assisting individuals in obtaining an abortion elsewhere. In order to best support the client's right to self-determination, the social worker should:

    A. Assist the client in exploring options and available resources to access abortion services, including those in neighboring states
    B. Provide the client with alternative resources such as adoption agencies and crisis pregnancy centers
    C. Explore the pros and cons of abortion with the client
    D. Refer the client for pastoral counseling

115. Parents of a 12-month old infant express concern that their child is not speaking enough. The infant is saying "mama" and "dada," but has not used any other words. In order to best assist this family, the social worker should:

    A. Reassure the parents that trying to say a few words besides "mama" and "dada" is a developmental milestone usually seen around 15 months
    B. Refer the infant for a neurological evaluation
    C. Request copies of the infant's medical records to see if any abnormalities have been discovered

D. Disclose the social worker's own history of delayed speech as an infant

116. A couple presents for relationship counseling and reports that recent instances of fighting have escalated into physical violence. To best assist this couple, the social worker should:

A. Explain to the couple that couples therapy is not recommended in relationships in which there is physical violence, and refer each partner for individual therapy
B. Meet with the couple for at least one session per week in order to ensure they make progress and avoid further violence
C. Utilize a dialectical behavior therapy approach in working with this couple
D. Make sure to use evidence-based practices in treating this couple given the severity of their difficulties

117. A client meets with a social worker after the client has just finalized a divorce. The client states he has no feelings about this and does not think there is anything to talk about. The social worker responds by pointing out that this was a significant event and that people would typically experience a range of emotions after a divorce. The social worker is most likely using the technique of:

A. Confrontation
B. Active listening
C. Countertransference
D. Reaction formation

118. A social worker meets with a 20-year-old client for an assessment. The client reports experiencing auditory and visual hallucinations as well as beliefs that the police are trying to catch him for a crime he did not commit. The client reports that these symptoms began 1 year ago and have made it difficult for him to work and to maintain relationships.

The client denies any substance use. Which of the following is the client's most likely DSM-5 diagnosis?

A. Schizophrenia
B. Major depressive disorder
C. Obsessive-compulsive disorder
D. Borderline personality disorder

119. A client meets with a social worker and reports that he has recently been feeling very tired during the day. He has also been sleeping approximately 10-12 hours each night. To best assist this client in determining the cause of his symptoms, the social worker should FIRST:

A. Refer the client for a psychiatric evaluation
B. Arrange for a clinic nurse to check the client's vital signs
C. Develop a treatment plan that includes cognitive behavioral therapy
D. Refer the client for a medical examination

120. The primary purpose of discharge planning is to:

A. Provide a placement setting for social work interns
B. Provide a clear social work role in a hospital facility
C. Ensure that clients' needs are met after they leave the facility
D. Reduce the facility's legal liability

121. A social worker is working with a client for anger management therapy. The client reports that last week he beat his child, who ended up fracturing a bone and needing to go to the hospital. The client expresses remorse and assures the social worker he will never do this again. The social worker should:

A. Report this incident to the state's mandated reporter hotline
B. Thank the client for sharing this and assure the client that this information will remain confidential

C. Document the issue in the client's record and return to focusing on treatment goals

D. Ask a supervisor whether or not this incident needs to be reported

122. A social worker has been meeting with a client who has major depressive disorder. After several months of severe depressive symptoms, the client comes into the session and reports suddenly feeling better. The client states that his mood has improved now that he realizes there is a way out of this depression and that he will not have to suffer forever. What should the social worker do NEXT?

A. Conduct a suicide risk assessment

B. Begin the termination process

C. Reduce the frequency of sessions

D. Provide psychoeducation regarding depressive episodes

123. In accordance with the Health Insurance Portability and Accountability Act, social workers have an obligation to:

A. Keep clients records confidential and obtain consent before releasing records

B. Warn and protect individuals who are being threatened by a client

C. Refer clients for psychological testing to obtain diagnostic clarification

D. Inform clients of which insurance plans the social worker accepts as a participating provider

124. A client reports having committed a violent crime against another adult for which he was not prosecuted. He then asks the social worker, "You're not going to turn me in, are you?" The social worker should FIRST:

A. Report the crime to the authorities

B. Contact the victim to ascertain their wishes regarding prosecution

C. Reassure the client about confidentiality guidelines

D. Explore the client's feelings about the disclosure

125. A social worker meets with a client who has dysregulated emotions and chaotic interpersonal relationships. As part of the treatment plan, the social worker recommends a skills group that covers mindfulness, emotion regulation, interpersonal effectiveness, and distress tolerance. The group most likely uses techniques of:

A. Dialectical behavior therapy
B. Acceptance and commitment therapy
C. Interpersonal psychotherapy
D. Psychodynamic psychotherapy

126. A social worker in private practice is working with a client who suddenly lost his insurance and cannot pay for services. The client is a Reiki healer and suggests he provide Reiki services to the therapist in exchange for therapy sessions. The social worker should:

A. Accept the exchange so the client can continue treatment
B. Accept the exchange on the condition that the Reiki sessions do not involve physical touch
C. Decline the exchange and terminate services immediately
D. Decline the exchange and work with the client on termination and referral to free or low cost services in the community

127. A 16-year old client meets with a social worker after being referred by his school after getting into multiple physical fights. The social worker recommends that the client join a martial arts program. The social worker's technique is most likely based on an understanding of:

A. Conversion
B. Repression
C. Transference
D. Sublimation

128. A college student visits the school counseling center during finals week and reports that he recently began wetting his bed. The student is most likely experiencing:

A. Repression
B. Regression
C. Transference
D. Projection

129. You are a social worker on an inpatient hospital unit. You meet with a client for an assessment, and the client states that he does not believe you can help him. He states that you have never been in his situation and cannot possibly understand. He expresses that he would like to decline the social work assessment. What should you do FIRST?

A. Inform the client of your academic and professional credentials
B. Acknowledge the client's feelings
C. Ask the client if he would prefer to meet with a different social worker
D. Explain to the client that a social work assessment is required by hospital policy

130. A social worker is at church and sees a former client in the pews. How should the social worker handle this situation?

A. The social worker should leave the church immediately
B. The social worker should approach and greet the client
C. The social worker should behave as they normally would in church
D. The social worker should make efforts to avoid the client

131. Which of the following would be considered an example of secondary prevention?

A. Helping a client with a recent injury obtain workplace accommodations to reduce the risk of exacerbating their condition.

B. Providing vaccines against COVID-19 to the general population

C. Designing a public service campaign encouraging the use of sunscreen to prevent skin cancer

D. Providing palliative care to patients with terminal illness

132. A client has been meeting with a social worker for the past 6 months for help with his anxiety. In recent weeks, the client has been reporting a significant reduction of symptoms. He is using the skills he learned in therapy and has described no other treatment goals. The social worker should:

A. Begin the termination process

B. Refer the client to a different social worker

C. Suggest that the client take a brief vacation from therapy

D. Change the treatment modality to a different therapeutic approach

133. You are a school social worker in a public elementary school. A teacher refers a student who has displayed disruptive behaviors in the classroom setting. The best way to assess the student's school behavior would be to:

A. Conduct a home visit

B. Meet with the student in the social worker's office

C. Observe the student's behavior in the classroom

D. Meet with the student's parents

134. According to Mary Richmond's concept of a "social diagnosis":

A. Poverty and social exclusion are the product of an individual's interactions with their social environment.

B. Individuals' problems are the result of mental health disorders.

C. Mental health problems are caused by the client's mother.

D. Psychotherapeutic interventions should be determined based on the client's social identities.

135. With regard to continuing education, which of the following is correct?

 A. Social workers have an ethical responsibility to review professional literature and participate in continuing education activities.
 B. Social workers must pursue continuing education activities only if required by their employer to do so.
 C. Social workers must pursue continuing education activities only if required by a licensing board to do so.
 D. Social workers are not required to participate in continuing education activities, but may do so if they wish.

136. A client is referred for a medication evaluation. The client reports that he has periods of feeling down, depressed, and hopeless, but that recently he has been staying up all night, gambling, making large purchases, and getting into frequent arguments. Based on the client's report, he is most likely to be prescribed which of the following medications?

 A. Ritalin
 B. Valium
 C. Lithium
 D. Prilosec

137. In conducting a community needs assessment, you survey local residents about their likelihood of visiting a second location of a social service agency where you work. Residents are asked to indicate on a scale of 1 to 10, with 10 being the highest, how likely they are to make use of the second location. The most common response is a 6. This data point represents the:

 A. Mean

B. Median

C. Mode

D. Range

138. You are working with a client who has a different cultural background and beliefs than you do. To best assist this client, you should:

A. Seek training and education opportunities to improve your cultural competency and knowledge about the client's culture

B. Refer the client to a social worker that has the same background as the client

C. Ask the client to tell you more about their culture

D. Ignore the cultural differences in order to stay on task

139. You are a social work supervisor in an agency. One of your supervisees reports feeling frustrated by her clients' lack of progress. She states that she feels ineffective and does not know if she can continue doing this work. The supervisee is most likely experiencing:

A. Secondary trauma

B. Transference

C. Reaction formation

D. Burnout

140. A hospital social worker is placed on a unit for patients with COVID-19. After several weeks of working on this unit, the social worker reports feeling increased irritability, being easily startled, and having nightmares about death and dying. The social worker is most likely experiencing:

A. Countertransference

B. Projective identification

C. Secondary trauma

D. Compassion fatigue

141. A client is terminating treatment after meeting with a social worker for psychotherapy for the past two years. At the end of the termination session, the client asks if she can hug the social worker. The social worker should:

A. Consider the appropriateness of physical contact with this client and handle the request in a way that conveys clear, appropriate, and culturally sensitive boundaries
B. Explain to the client that physical contact would not be ethical
C. Tell the client that her request is inappropriate
D. Remind the client of the professional nature of the relationship

142. Before meeting with a client for the first time, a social worker types the client's name into Google in order to obtain background information. This action by the social worker is:

A. Ethical because the information obtained is publicly available
B. Ethical because the social worker did not disclose this information to a third party
C. Unethical because the social worker did not obtain the client's consent before conducting the Google search
D. Unethical because the social worker did not first discuss the search with a supervisor

143. A client is referred to you through his employee assistance program. The program covers up to five sessions of counseling, but based on your assessment you believe the client requires longer term treatment. To best serve this client, you should:

A. Use the five sessions as efficiently as possible to try to meet the client's goals
B. Determine if the client can access additional sessions using his insurance coverage and/or other resources
C. Work out a bartering arrangement with the client

D. Meet with the client for as many sessions as needed, but only document the first five sessions

144. A client reports that he has noticed negative effects from his alcohol use and wishes to cut down on his drinking. He does not meet the DSM-5 criteria for Alcohol Use Disorder and does not wish to eliminate alcohol entirely. To best help this client, the social worker should:

A. Inform the client that the social worker can only help if the client is willing to stop drinking
B. Refer the client to Alcoholics Anonymous
C. Assist the client in setting specific goals related to his alcohol use and develop a plan to work toward those goals
D. Tell the client that he does not need to reduce his drinking since he does not meet DSM-5 criteria for Alcohol Use Disorder

145. Self-care is BEST defined as:

A. Activities and practices to reduce stress and maintain health and well-being
B. Regular appointments for manicures, pedicures, and massages
C. A daily exercise routine
D. Use of social work interventions on oneself

146. An elementary school student frequently gets up from his seat during class lessons. In an effort to eliminate this behavior, the teacher subtracts 5 minutes of recess time for every instance in which the student gets up from his seat. The teacher is attempting to use:

A. Positive reinforcement
B. Negative reinforcement
C. Positive punishment
D. Negative punishment

147. An 68 year old client reports experiencing a depressed mood. He tells the social worker that this began a few years ago, but had never been a problem earlier in his life. He reports reflecting back on the years of his life and struggling to find meaning in his experiences. Based on Erikson's stages of psychosocial development, the client is experiencing difficulties with:

A. Identity vs. Role Confusion
B. Intimacy vs. Isolation
C. Generativity vs. Stagnation
D. Integrity vs. Despair

148. A client is in psychoanalytic treatment with a clinical social worker. The social worker makes an interpretation of a dream that a client has described, and the client abruptly changes the subject. The social worker will most likely view this behavior as:

A. Resistance
B. Countertransference
C. Transference
D. Breakthrough

149. A social worker asks a client to imagine that a miracle occurs one night while the client is sleeping, in which all of the client's problems have disappeared. The social worker asks the client to describe what they would first notice that would tell them things had gotten better. The social worker is most likely using techniques of:

A. Solution-Focused Therapy
B. Psychoanalysis
C. Interpersonal Psychotherapy
D. Eye Movement Desensitization and Reprocessing

150. An agency administrator puts significant effort into building a sense of cohesion among the staff. She delegates responsibilities to

others on her leadership team in order to create a culture of shared leadership. Staff feel comfortable approaching this administrator with their concerns, and she has created a reputation of working toward solutions when problems arise. This administrator is most likely using the organizational management approach of:

A. Systems Theory
B. Scientific Management Theory
C. Structural-Functional Theory
D. Human Relations Theory

Practice Test Answers

1. D
2. D
3. D
4. A
5. A
6. C
7. A
8. D
9. A
10. D
11. B
12. A
13. A
14. A
15. B
16. D
17. B
18. A
19. C
20. D
21. A
22. B
23. D

24. A
25. C
26. B
27. A
28. C
29. C
30. B
31. D
32. D
33. A
34. D
35. C
36. A
37. B
38. A
39. C
40. D
41. B
42. C
43. D
44. D
45. A
46. C
47. B
48. D
49. A
50. A
51. D
52. B
53. A
54. A
55. A
56. D

57. A
58. B
59. C
60. A
61. B
62. A
63. D
64. A
65. B
66. B
67. A
68. A
69. D
70. B
71. D
72. A
73. D
74. D
75. B
76. D
77. A
78. A
79. A
80. A
81. D
82. D
83. A
84. A
85. B
86. A
87. C
88. A
89. D

90. A
91. A
92. A
93. A
94. C
95. C
96. B
97. A
98. C
99. A
100. A
101. B
102. B
103. A
104. A
105. C
106. B
107. C
108. A
109. C
110. A
111. B
112. B
113. B
114. A
115. A
116. A
117. A
118. A
119. D
120. C
121. A
122. A

123. A
124. C
125. A
126. D
127. D
128. B
129. B
130. C
131. A
132. A
133. C
134. A
135. A
136. C
137. C
138. A
139. D
140. C
141. A
142. C
143. B
144. C
145. A
146. D
147. D
148. A
149. A
150. D

Practice Test Answer Explanations

1. **D.** Ego integrity vs. despair refers to the eighth and final stage in Erik Erikson's psychosocial stages of development, and takes place from approximately the age of 65 years through to the end of life. In this stage, individuals experience the conflict of determining whether they have lived a meaningful life.

2. **D.** There is actually a positive relationship between spirituality and mental health. While multiple models exist to explain the ways in which religious and spiritual beliefs affect human behavior, the major models all tend to move through the stages of an egocentric state, to a conformist state, to a universalistic state. Spirituality can help individuals cope with events that seem to be out of their control, and in this way spirituality is positively correlated with mental health outcomes.

3. **D.** The psychological defense of undoing refers to efforts to cancel or remove an unwanted behavior or thought by engaging in behavior contrary to the original behavior or thought. In this case, the client is attempting to "undo" his guilt about not walking his friend's dog by doing something contrary, making a donation to support the care of other animals.

4. **A.** In social work, feminist theory provides a framework for understanding women's experiences in a patriarchal society, as well as a way to look at gendered roles, expectations, and experiences as they impact everyone. In this case, the social worker challenges the couple's apparent assumptions regarding the roles of the husband and wife in their marriage.

5. **A.** The biopsychosocial assessment that serves as a foundation of social work practice is most aligned with person-in-environment theory. According to this theory, people are significantly impacted by their surroundings, and human behavior can be understood in the context of people's interactions with their environment. Similarly, the biopsychosocial model considers biological, psychological, and social factors to understand a person's behavior and emotional experience.

6. **C.** According to Tuckman's model of group development, groups experience the stages of forming, storming, norming, and performing. Tuckman later added a fifth stage to the model, adjourning (also known as mourning), in which the group has completed its purpose and group members separate. In the storming stage, group members must resolve conflict and tension that arises as they form opinions about each other and question actions and decisions.

7. **A.** Crisis intervention is a short-term model for assisting individuals affected by physical, mental, and behavioral distress to return to stability and prevent negative long-term impacts of the crisis. Crisis intervention is time limited as it is an emergency response specifically to help the person return to a state of equilibrium.

8. **D.** According to resilience theory, individuals' assets and resources such as self-esteem, self-efficacy, and social support counteract risk exposure to support positive outcomes. Because of resilience,

clients can achieve healthy outcomes in spite of negative circumstances. Even when faced with risk, people can grow and adapt, mobilizing resources to improve their situation. Social problems are understood as creating risk not due to individual pathology but rather due to environmental and structural factors.

9. **A.** According to the DSM-5, persistent complex bereavement disorder is diagnosed only after 12 months have passed in adults, or 6 months in children, since the death of someone with whom the bereaved person had a close relationship. This time frame is intended to distinguish between normal grief and persistent grief.

10. **D.** According to psychodynamic theories, personality develops based on childhood experiences and involves automatic, unconscious mental processes. People use defense mechanisms to protect the conscious mind from overwhelming or uncomfortable feelings. Conditioning and reinforcement are components of behavioral, rather than psychodynamic, theories.

11. **B.** Social workers are considered mandated reporters and must contact their state's designated reporting agency any time that they suspect child abuse or neglect. A report must be made regardless of a supervisor's assessment and even if the social worker does not have enough information to ascertain whether or not abuse has occurred.

12. **A.** Gender identity refers to a person's sense of their own gender, while gender expression refers to the ways in which a person expresses their gender identity such as through appearance, clothing, and behavior.

13. **A.** Bisexuality refers to the experience of being attracted to more than one gender. This can include both romantic attraction and sexual attraction, and the term can also refer to sexual behavior.

Bisexual people experience discrimination and misunderstanding both within and outside the LGBTQ community. One false stereotype that bisexual people often face is that bisexuality is a temporary phase and that they are simply figuring out whether they are truly straight or gay. While sexuality is indeed fluid and can change over time, bisexuality is no less valid than straight and gay identities.

14. **A.** Social justice refers to the belief that every person deserves equal rights and opportunities. While one social justice related concept is equality, giving every person the same rights and resources, a challenge to this idea comes from the concept of equity. Equity refers to the allocation of resources and opportunities based on the needs of individuals and groups, taking into account the privileges already in place in order to create equal outcomes. In social work, social justice is important at all levels, including micro, mezzo, and macro practice. There are many theories of social justice, including critical race theory, but this is not a complete definition of social justice.

15. **B.** Community organizing refers to the process by which people in the same geographic area or with common problems or interests come together to promote their shared interests. Social workers engaged in community organizing empower people to develop and improve their communities.

16. **D.** A mental status examination is a standard tool that clinicians use to assess a client's cognitive and behavioral functioning. Components of the mental status examination include appearance, behavior, speech, mood, affect, perception, thought content, thought process, insight, judgment, and cognition.

17. **B.** Clients have a legal right to access their records, and the NASW Code of Ethics requires that social workers provide clients with

reasonable access to their records. The Code of Ethics further states that, when social workers have a concern that access to records could cause clients serious misunderstanding or harm, social workers should provide assistance in interpreting the records. It is only in exceptional circumstances of potential for serious harm that social workers can withhold or limit clients' access to their records.

18. **A.** This question is asking about research design, with the research methods represented in terms of the timing of measurements taken. "A" refers to measurements taken at baseline and "B" refers to measurements taken during treatment. In this case, an A-B-A design, which can also be called a reversal design, involves taking a baseline measurement, initiating the intervention (with measurements taken), and then discontinuing the intervention and measuring the new baseline.

19. **C.** Dialectical behavior therapy is the treatment method with the strongest empirical evidence for treatment of borderline personality disorder. DBT is a type of cognitive behavioral therapy that involves individual psychotherapy, group skills training, telephone coaching, and therapist participation on a consultation team.

20. **D.** The NASW Code of Ethics includes standards on cultural competence and diversity, which include that social workers should demonstrate awareness and cultural humility, engage in critical self-reflection, and obtain education about social diversity oppression. Social workers can and do work with clients whose cultural backgrounds are different from their own.

21. **A.** Harm reduction refers to a public health philosophy and method of interventions that seek to reduce potential harms of drug use rather than seeking to stop individuals' drug use. On the

other hand, 12-step programs and abstinence-based substance use treatment programs are focused on stopping use and preventing relapse.

22. **B.** Active listening refers to a communication process in which the listener devotes their full attention to what they are hearing in order to understand the person who is speaking. Active listening includes techniques such as listening without judgment, avoiding interruption, repeating back what the listener has heard, and asking clarifying questions.

23. **D.** Role plays are an effective technique for improving clients' interpersonal skills, improving communication, and teaching empathy. Role play is used with clients, in supervision, as well as in social work education. While role play techniques often require preparation and explanation, this is not a clinical benefit.

24. **A.** Social workers are often in the role of helping clients to manage feelings, including anger. Relaxation skills help clients to create for themselves an environment of safety and comfort. Learning how to put situations into a larger perspective facilitates acceptance and helps clients to decrease the intensity of anger. Similarly, learning how to walk away from upsetting situations helps clients to set and maintain boundaries in order to avoid triggers.

25. **C.** One of the most valuable aspects of group work is the support that groups members receive from one another and the realization that they are not alone. Group members may be hesitant to share in session, and so it is important that the social worker support clients in opening up to the group.

26. **B.** According to the NASW Code of Ethics, social workers are obligated to engage in social and political action in order to support

the equal access of all people to the resources, services, and opportunities that they need. Further, the Code of Ethics states that social workers should support social and cultural diversity and act to prevent and eliminate exploitation and discrimination.

27. **A.** Freud's stages of psychosexual development include the oral, anal, phallic, latent, and genital stages. The anal stage takes place between the ages of 18 months to three years. During this age range, as toilet training takes place, Freud conceived of pleasure as being derived through the control of bowel and bladder movement.

28. **C.** An important part of service planning and provision, the needs assessment is a tool for identifying the needs and resources of a community in order to pursue community improvement and change. A needs assessment engages stakeholders in the community to identify and respond to specific social problems.

29. **C.** Competence is listed as one of the core values in the NASW Code of Ethics. The Code of Ethics states, "Social workers practice within their areas of competence and develop and enhance their professional expertise."

30. **B.** The NASW Code of Ethics lists the following core values in its section on ethical principles of the social work profession: service, social justice, dignity and worth of the person, importance of human relationships, integrity, and competence.

31. **D.** Networking is an important way in which social workers share resources and expertise, establish professional relationships with other clinicians, and identify candidates for job openings. Social workers should not become involved in business opportunities with clients as this would create dual relationships.

32. **D.** Quality assurance in social work refers to methods used to ensure the clients receive services that meet established standards. Some steps taken for the purpose of quality assurance include incorporating standards throughout an agency, gathering data and information on program and service outcomes, and analyzing data for the purpose of making improvements.

33. **A.** Cost effectiveness analysis is used to assess the monetary cost of achieving non-monetary outcomes. For example, cost effectiveness analysis can compare one intervention to another, or one intervention to the status quo, in order to evaluate the dollar amount that is spent per unit of improved health or other social benefit.

34. **D.** According to the NASW Code of Ethics, when social workers have direct knowledge of a colleague's impairment, they should first consult with that colleague when feasible and assist the colleague in taking remedial action. Only if the colleague has not taken adequate steps to address the impairment should the social worker then take action through their employer, licensing board, or other organization.

35. **C.** An institutional review board is responsible for protecting the rights and welfare of human subjects in medical and behavioral research, approving and monitoring research activities within its jurisdiction, and ensuring that adequate measures are in place to protect privacy and confidentiality. Institutional review boards do not otherwise oversee educational or teaching functions.

36. **A.** Consent can only be given by those who have reached the legal age of consent, which is typically 18 years old. Assent refers to the agreement by an individual who is not able to give consent. Research with participants who are not capable of giving consent

requires that the researcher obtain the consent of the parent or legal guardian as well as the assent of the research subject.

37. **B.** Supervision in social work includes individual and group methods, as well as peer supervision (also called peer consultation). Social workers work with individuals, families, groups, organizations, communities, and society as a whole; however,, family intervention is not a model of supervision or consultation.

38. **A.** So-called "conversion therapy" intended to change an individual's sexual orientation has been found to be ineffective and harmful. According to the NASW Code of Ethics, social workers are responsible for promoting the well-being of clients. The Code of Ethics further states that "Social workers should obtain education about and demonstrate understanding of the nature of social diversity and oppression."

39. **C.** According to Maslow's hierarchy of needs, physiological needs are the most basic level and include those needs that are vital to survival such as food, air, water, shelter, and clothing. Sexual reproduction is included at this level as well since it is vital to human survival as a species.

40. **D.** Elisabeth Kubler-Ross' grief model includes the five stages of denial, anger, bargaining, depression, and acceptance. In the denial stage, individuals may believe that a terminal diagnosis or death is mistaken, and they may instead cling to a false reality. Kubler-Ross also states that people may deny the reality of their own inevitable death.

41. **B.** The problem-solving process, also known as the helping process, includes the stages (in this order) of engagement, assessment, planning, intervention, evaluation, and termination. Note that

the the evaluation stage refers to an evaluation of the outcomes of the intervention, not to a psychological evaluation of a client.

42. **C.** According to Piaget, children between the ages of 2 and 7 are in the preoperational stage of cognitive development. During the preoperational stage, children do not yet understand concrete logic. However, they are able to understand symbols and thus there is an increase in play and pretend. Role playing is also common during this period.

43. **D.** According to the NASW Code of Ethics, social workers are expected to routinely review professional literature and participate in continuing education related to social work practice. This may consist of in-service training and/or outside workshops. Clinical practice, such as conducting intake assessments and psychotherapy, does help social workers to strengthen their skills but is not considered a professional development activity.

44. **D.** Social workers are required to protect the confidentiality of client information. Social workers must protect written client records by keeping files in a secure location. When speaking with colleagues about shared clients, social workers should avoid discussing confidential information in public or semipublic areas. In addition, when disclosing information to third parties, even with client consent, social workers should share only the minimum amount of information needed for the purpose of the disclosure.

45. **A.** Transference refers to emotional reactions of a client that are redirected toward the therapist, while countertransference refers to the therapist's emotional reactions that are redirected toward a client. Transference and countertransference both include feelings that are related to an important figure in the individual's life that are then directed toward someone else (i.e., the therapist or client).

46. **C.** Time management refers to activities intended to increase effectiveness and productivity. It is used in both business and personal applications. Time management techniques include categorizing activities based on importance and urgency. Addressing only urgent issues does not take into account the extent to which these issues are the most important ones to focus on.

47. **B.** Compassion fatigue includes both emotional and physical exhaustion that inhibits one's capacity to empathize and feel compassion for others. It is caused by exposure to traumatic material and may have a sudden, rapid onset. Its symptoms can mirror those of post traumatic stress disorder.

48. **D.** Social transitions typically associated with late adulthood include retirement, widowhood, and grandparenthood. Eco-mapping, on the other hand, refers to the use of ecomaps, a visual tool for understanding an individual and their relationships to the outside world. Ecomaps help social workers to gather information that helps in understanding situations that may be contributing to a person's problems as well as resources and assets that can be used to improve the person's situation.

49. **A.** The concept of linked lives, a part of the life course perspective, describes the ways in which people in especially significant relationships with one another (i.e., parents and children) experience interconnected developmental trajectories. During infancy and early childhood, an individual's development is most connected with that of their parent or caregiver.

50. **A.** During adolescence and early adulthood, cognitive development continues as an individual further develops their capacity for foresight and abstract thinking. From a neurological perspective, this development is tied to the growing maturity of the frontal lobe.

51. **D.** As individuals develop from adolescence into early adulthood, they experience a number of key social transitions including employment, relationship formation, and independent living.

52. **B.** Scapegoating refers to the blaming of one person for the wrongdoings or faults of others. In family therapy, it is important for the therapist to help the family understand the ways in which they all participate in the problems of the identified scapegoat.

53. **A.** Sexual paraphilias involve the association of otherwise non-sexual objects with pleasurable sexual activity. This process can be explained through classical conditioning, as sexual arousal becomes a conditioned response to a conditioned stimulus.

54. **A.** John Bowlby is known for his work in attachment theory. Based on his hypothesis that infants' reactions to separation from, and reconnection with, caregivers were evolutionary mechanisms for survival, Bowlby developed his theory of an "attachment behavioral system." Based on this theory, infants react based on patterns of secure attachment, anxious attachment, or avoidant attachment. Later, other researchers added the fourth style of disorganized attachment.

55. **A.** Attachment refers to a strong emotional bond that an infant forms with their caregiver, as well as the process by which the infant forms this bond. Attachment theory was first developed by John Bowlby based on a hypothesis that the ways in which infants react to separation from their caregivers, as well as reconnection after separation, are driven by evolutionary mechanisms for survival.

56. **D.** Abraham Maslow theorized that people focus on meeting their most basic needs and then progress upward, fulfilling each level until they can potentially reach self-actualization. According

to Maslow's hierarchy of needs, the most basic level consists of physiological needs including food, shelter, and warmth.

57. **A.** Caregiver stress is a common phenomenon among adult children caring for their aging parents. Individuals caring for an elderly, disabled, or injured family member may neglect their own physical and emotional health. As a result of the strain of caregiving, individuals may experience physical, emotional, and mental exhaustion.

58. **B.** As a part of cultural competence in working with LGBTQ clients, it is important that social workers acknowledge clients' pronouns and use the pronouns requested when referring to the client. According to published research, use of a chosen name and pronouns reduces depressive symptoms and suicidal ideation among transgender youth.

59. **C.** Narrative gerontology is an approach that uses the idea of a person's life as a story in order to help people add value to their lives. By creating and maintaining their personal narrative, individuals can make sense of their experiences, construct stories that validate their identities, pass along information, and develop their sense of self-worth.

60. **A.** While healthy defenses (also known as mature defense mechanisms) support an individual in conserving their energy to meet the demands of daily life responsibilities, neurotic defenses impede the individual's ability to manage their life and relationships.

61. **B.** Parentification is a type of role reversal in which a child takes on emotional or practical responsibilities for their parents or for other family members. Essentially, the child has to act as a parent to their own parent, to a sibling or siblings, or to another person close to them. While parentification is not always maladaptive

(indeed, it is said that the parentified child goes to social work school), parentification has been linked to a number of adverse impacts.

62. **A.** In order to obtain medical services related to gender transition, clients may require a letter from a mental health professional attesting to a gender dysphoria diagnosis, capacity to consent, and/or medical necessity. Providing these letters of support is an important aspect of comprehensive care for transgender, gender non-conforming, and non-binary clients.

63. **D.** Occupational burnout is a common experience among social workers and includes symptoms such as physical exhaustion, increased irritability, and feeling ineffective in one's work. Scheduling of vacations and taking personal time off represents one way in which social workers can combat the risk of burnout.

64. **A.** Person-in-environment theory is an approach to understanding an individual's lived experience in the context of the systems with which they interact. Person-in-environment theory is a key practice-guiding philosophy in the field of social work. A person's experiences in transaction with their environment shapes how they see the world, how they think, and why they respond to situations in the way that they do.

65. **B.** It is very common for social workers to experience burnout, even if they practice self-care or have other resilience factors. Occupational burnout has many causes, including factors related to client work, organizational problems, and other contextual factors in the individual's life.

66. **B.** The eco-structural therapy is a model of family therapy that seeks to improve the interactions between family members. In this model, families seeking help are connected to other families

in similar situations, in order to provide mutual support and an increased sense of community.

67. **A.** Social workers have an ethical obligation to protect client confidentiality. When served with a subpoena, the social worker should object to it by filing a "Motion to Quash." A subpoena can be issued by a judge, a court clerk, or an attorney. While a subpoena cannot be ignored, it does not mean that the issuer has authority to compel the release of records unless it is accompanied by a court order signed by a judge.

68. **A.** The decision in *Tarasoff v. Regents of the University of California* established legal precedent for the principle that mental health professionals have a duty to warn individuals who are threatened with physical harm by a client. Duty to warn is thus one of the exceptions to social worker - client confidentiality.

69. **D.** Client information is to be kept confidential indefinitely, even after a client is deceased, with limited exceptions for cases in which the client poses a danger to themself or others, or in cases of suspected child abuse or elder abuse.

70. **B.** An ethical dilemma refers to a situation in which a decision must be made in the face of two or more conflicting ethical values or principles. When faced with an ethical dilemma, a social worker must consider the multiple ethical issues at stake in order to determine the best course of action.

71. **D.** Restorative justice is an approach to justice that involves a meeting between the affected parties, and at times individuals from the larger community. In this approach, there is a focus on accountability and collaboration in order for the offending party to repair the harm that was done.

72. **A.** The NASW Code of Ethics states that social workers should engage in social and political action to support equal access to resources and opportunities for all people, and to advocate for policies that improve social conditions. Social workers are required to take action to expand choice and opportunity for all people, with a focus on vulnerable and oppressed groups.

73. **D.** In a therapeutic relationship, erotic transference is is a phenomenon in which a client shifts erotic feelings and desires from past attachments to the therapist. The social worker in this case must maintain appropriate boundaries while exploring the client's feelings.

74. **D.** Assertiveness training involves teaching clients skills for dealing with frustrating situations effectively, making requests, and refusing requests when it would be helpful to do so. Assertiveness skills are not intended to be used for the purpose of engaging in unhelpful conflict, but rather are to help clients navigate situations in an effective way.

75. **B.** In many ways, social policy determines the ways in which social work is practiced. This is one reason that social workers should engage in social and political action, as policy decisions affect clients as well as social workers in many aspects of direct and indirect social work practice.

76. **D.** Active listening is a set of skills for creating a shared mutual understanding between a speaker and listener. Active listening involves listening without interrupting, asking open-ended questions, paying attention to non-verbal cues such as body language and facial expressions, and reflecting back what is heard.

77. **A.** Before intervening with this client system (the organization and its staff), it is important that the social worker understand

their needs. A needs assessment will help the social worker understand current gaps in order to determine what types of training will be helpful. After conducting the needs assessment, the social worker can then make a plan for staff training that meets the needs of the staff and organization.

78. **A.** Empirical research refers to research based on observed and measured experiences. Qualitative, quantitative, and mixed methods research are all types of empirical research. Empirical research is conducted through a variety of funding streams, including government sources.

79. **A.** The task-centered model of practice is a short-term, problem solving approach to help clients achieve their goals and find solutions to specific problems. In the task-centered model, behavioral approaches are used to promote completion of a task and to produce measurable outcomes.

80. **A.** Evidence-based practice involves the use of research and data to guide policy and practice decisions. While some manualized treatments are considered evidence-based, evidence-based practice is a broader concept referring to the use of practice methods that are proven to be effective for particular problems. Cognitive-behavioral therapy is one such practice for certain disorders, but would not be used with all clients.

81. **D.** Qualitative research involves the collection of non-numerical data such as observations, interviews, and descriptive questionnaires. Quantitative research involves the collection of numerical data such as rating scales and other statistical metrics. Both qualitative and quantitative research are empirical methods, and one is not necessarily of a higher quality than the other.

82. **D.** Qualitative research methods utilize inductive reasoning and therefore allow the researcher to surface those phenomena that are central to the participants' lived experience. The researcher can use the data collected to generate new theories or revise previous theories based on what is learned from the people most affected.

83. **A.** In single-subject design, the subject serves as their own control rather than being compared to a separate control group. There are different types of single-subject design in which measurements are collected at baseline and/or during or after an intervention.

84. **A.** Structural family therapy was developed by Salvador Minuchin and seeks to address problems in functioning within a family system. In this model, the therapist joins with the family system, allowing the therapist to understand the family's unwritten rules.

85. **B.** Executive functioning refers to a set of cognitive processes and skills that individuals use to plan for an carry out their goals. People with attention-deficit/hyperactivity disorder (ADHD) often struggle with one or more executive functions, making it difficult to start or finish tasks, but executive functioning is a broader concept impacting people with and without ADHD.

86. **A.** Dialectical behavior therapy includes a skills training group that teaches skills for mindfulness, emotion regulation, inter-personal effectiveness, and distress tolerance. Mindfulness skills are used to improve clients' emotion regulation and decrease rumination.

87. **C.** Trauma-informed care is described in several different theoretical models, but all include common components of safety and stabilization, mourning and remembrance, and reconnection and reintegration. Avoidance and reexperiencing are categories of

symptoms experienced by individuals with post-traumatic stress disorder.

88. **A.** Self-disclosure, in general, is not an unethical practice in social work. In fact, it can be beneficial to clients in some cases. However, self-disclosure can also at times can be harmful to clients, and can potentially indicate a boundary crossing or boundary violation. Self-disclosure should only be used when it will clearly be of benefit to the client, and social workers should seek supervision or consultation regarding the use of self-disclosure.

89. **D.** Types of advocacy in which social workers engage include self advocacy, case advocacy, and class (also called cause) advocacy. Self advocacy refers to speaking up for oneself and one's own needs. Case advocacy refers to efforts on behalf of a client to get their needs met. In class (cause) advocacy, the social worker engages in systemic efforts to help a larger group or community.

90. **A.** Anorexia nervosa is an eating disorder in which individuals restrict the types of found and amount of calories that they consume each day. Individuals with anorexia are often concerned with maintaining a low body weight, and may have a distorted body image.

91. **A.** Person-centered therapy, also called client-centered therapy, is an approach developed by Carl Rogers. Person-centered therapy is based on the key principles of empathy and unconditional positive regard. Rogers defines unconditional positive regard as caring for the client as a separate person and with permission to have their own feelings and experiences.

92. **A.** According to the *NASW Code of Ethics*, social workers should take reasonable steps to protect electronic communications,

including safeguards such as encryption, firewalls, and passwords, in order to protect client confidentiality.

93. **A.** The client is describing a manic episode, and has mentioned a history of depressive episodes as well. This indicates a likely diagnosis of Bipolar I disorder. In Bipolar II disorder, on the other hand, individuals experience hypomanic episodes, which are less severe and do not negatively impact work or social functioning. Because of this manic episode, he would not be diagnosed with major depressive disorder.

94. **C.** In acceptance and commitment therapy (ACT), clients learn acceptance and mindfulness strategies as well as strategies for commitment and for changing behavior. Clients are taught to reflect on their personal values in order to behave in ways consistent with these values. Acceptance is utilized to help clients cope with negative thoughts, feelings, and experiences.

95. **C.** This case example describes a client with symptoms likely consistent with borderline personality disorder. The treatment with the strongest empirical evidence for helping clients with borderline personality disorder is dialectical behavior therapy, which includes individual sessions as well as a skills training group, telephone coaching, and therapist participation on a consultation team.

96. **B.** Forensic social work is a field of social work practice in which social workers are involved with legal systems, which may include civil or criminal cases. Forensic social workers may be involved with cases relating to parental rights, juvenile and adult justice, corrections, and involuntary or mandated treatment.

97. **A.** The terms sympathy and empathy are often confused, even as distinctions between them are significant. Sympathy refers to

one person sharing the feelings of another. For example, one may express their sympathy -- their experience of sadness -- when another person is grieving. Empathy, on the other hand, refers to the imagination or understanding of how another person may feel, even when the person showing empathy may not experience those same feelings. Empathic responding is an important aspect of a helping relationship.

98. **C.** The Rorschach test is a projective psychological test that involves the client's interpretation of ambiguous inkblots for the assessment of personality traits and emotional functioning.

99. **A.** Based on Tuckman's model of group development, groups experience the stages of forming, storming, norming, and performing. Tuckman later added a fifth stage to the model, adjourning (also called the mourning stage), in which the group has completed its purpose and group members separate.

100. **A.** A program's effectiveness will be measured in terms of its goals, so identifying the goals of the program is the first step. Following this, the social worker would define measurable outcomes and then utilize qualitative and/or quantitative methods, which may include a process evaluation.

101. **B.** This case example may include a client who is experiencing intimate partner violence. In such cases, it is important that the social worker has the opportunity to assess the client's situation by speaking directly with the client without the partner present. This way, the client is more likely to answer questions openly without fear of the partner's reaction, which can allow the social worker to then assist the client with safety planning and resources if appropriate.

102. **B.** In order to address the needs of the Native American community in this area, the social worker must first find out what the needs are. Through a needs assessment, the social worker can find out about current unmet needs and gaps in services. Following the needs assessment, the social worker can advocate for services to fill these gaps and address unmet needs.

103. **A.** Engagement is the first step in the helping process. When working with a community, engagement involves immersing oneself into the community, establishing relationships, and beginning to understand existing community dynamics. Meeting with community leaders might be a part of this process, but might not come first and would not be sufficient. Following the engagement phase, the social worker may work in collaboration with community members to create goals and objectives, and to develop an action plan.

104. **A.** Carol Gilligan found that Kohlberg's theory of moral development was based on male norms in which males respond to moral dilemmas using abstract concepts such as justice, fairness, and equality. Gilligan provides an alternative view, known as the care perspective, which is based on her analysis that females respond to moral dilemmas based on interpersonal obligations, as they are concerned with how their decisions will affect others.

105. **C.** The student in this example is exhibiting conventional moral thinking, in which being good means following the rules. The idea that rules can be broken based on ethical principles would require post-conventional moral thinking.

106. **B.** Narrative therapy is a psychotherapeutic model that helps clients to develop new life stories while identifying their values and the skills that they bring to their lives. It is based on the idea that

people make meaning through how they interpret (i.e., how they would narrate) their experiences.

107. **C.** Rationalization is a defense mechanism in which the individual seeks to provide an explanation for their behavior. In this case, the client had failed to complete assigned tasks and was fired as a result. To cope with the reality of having lost his job due to his own failings, the client states that he is glad to be done working and had been planning to retire soon anyway.

108. **A.** Gender identity refers to a person's felt sense of being male, female, non-binary, or any other gender, while biological sex refers to a person's physical traits associated with being male, female, and/or intersex. Gender identity is an aspect of a person's experience whether or not they identify as LGBTQ, and can be the same as, or different from, the person's biological sex.

109. **C.** Positive reinforcement is a concept in operant conditioning that explains the impact of an added stimulus in making a behavior continue to occur. In this case, the client's suicidal gestures are reinforced by the response of her family members. For the client's condition to improve, it will be important that she find ways to receive positive reinforcement during times when she is not suicidal.

110. **A.** The client's most likely DSM-5 diagnosis is major depressive disorder. According to the DSM-5, diagnosis of major depressive disorder requires the occurrence of one or more major depressive episodes. A major depressive episode lasts for 2 weeks or longer and includes symptoms such as depressed mood, loss of interest or pleasure in activities, weight gain or weight loss, sleep disturbance, speeding or slowing down of muscle movement, loss of energy or fatigue, feelings of worthlessness, difficulty thinking or concentrating, and thoughts of death or dying.

111. **B.** According to the *NASW Code of Ethics*, social workers who become aware of a colleague's impairment should consult directly with the colleague and assist them in remediating the impairment. Only if the colleague has not taken adequate steps to address the impairment, and if the impairment interferes with the colleague's practice, should a social worker take action through other channels such as the employer or licensing body.

112. **B.** Telemental health services provide certain advantages, especially in offering access to clients who live in areas with limited mental health services. To provide telemental health services, social workers must consider licensure requirements, especially if clients are located in different states. It is important to obtain informed consent from clients that specifically addresses the risks and benefits of this service. Telemental health services are not the same as in-person services, and require special consideration.

113. **B.** While social workers must keep client information confidential, there are exceptions to confidentiality and circumstances in which it is necessary to break confidentiality. Social workers should discuss with clients their policies regarding confidentiality as well as limits to confidentiality. Additionally, in group settings, social workers should inform clients that they cannot guarantee that group members will keep information private.

114. **A.** According to the *NASW Code of Ethics*, social workers' primary responsibility is to their clients, and social workers must respect and promote their clients' right to self-determination. This involves helping clients to identify and clarify their goals. However, in this case it is already clear that the client wishes to obtain an abortion, and so the social worker should assist the client in accessing abortion care.

115. **A.** While the parents are expressing concern, there is no indication of any developmental delay for this infant. In fact, the infant's use of "mama" and "dada" is appropriate for the age of 12 months. The social worker's role in this case is to provide psychoeducation for the parents, reassuring them that the use of a few additional words is typically seen around 15 months of age.

116. **A.** Social workers should not provide couples therapy when there is physical violence in the relationship, as therapy can create additional risk for the victim as difficult emotions are surfaced in session. Additionally, couples therapy typically uses a premise of equal responsibility for problems in the relationship system, which would not be appropriate for an abusive relationship in which there is a pattern of power and control.

117. **A.** Confrontation is a therapeutic technique in which the social worker gently highlights contradictions or ambiguity. In this case, the client has just gone through a divorce and yet is stating he does not think there is anything to talk about. He states he has no feelings about it, even as a divorce is a significant life event. The therapist's use of confrontation highlights this contradiction in order to help the client address his reactions to the divorce.

118. **A.** The client's most likely DSM-5 diagnosis is schizophrenia. According to the DSM-5 criteria, schizophrenia is diagnosed when symptoms have lasted for 1 month or longer. Symptoms must include at least two of these 5 symptoms: delusions, hallucinations, disorganized speech, disorganized or catatonic behavior, or negative symptoms such as diminished emotional expression. At least one of the symptoms must be delusions, hallucinations, or disorganized speech.

119. **D.** In order to assess the client's symptoms, it is important to first rule out any possible medical cause of his fatigue and

hypersomnia. Any medical causes should first be addressed by a physician. If a physician determines that there is no medical cause, the social worker can then diagnose the client's condition and provide treatment.

120. **C.** The primary purpose of discharge planning is to ensure that the needs of a client will be met after they leave a facility. This is often a social work role, but discharge planning is also performed by nurses and case managers. While discharge planning does reduce a facility's legal liability, the primary purpose is to meet the needs of the client.

121. **A.** This incident must be reported to the state's mandated reporter hotline. Social workers are mandated reporters and are required to report any instance of suspected child abuse or neglect. This obligation is an exception to the confidentiality of client information, and is required regardless of input from supervisors or colleagues.

122. **A.** This client is at increased risk for suicide, and so a suicide risk assessment must be conducted. When individuals with depression report suddenly feeling better, this is sometimes because they have made the decision to end their life. This is an important warning sign that must be addressed immediately.

123. **A.** The Health Insurance Portability and Accountability Act, commonly known as HIPAA, requires healthcare providers to keep patient information confidential and to have safeguards in place to ensure the privacy and security of protected health information. Based on HIPAA regulations, social workers must keep protected health information secure and obtain consent for all disclosures that are not for the purposes of treatment, payment, or operations.

124. **C.** Disclosure of a past crime, regardless of the severity, is not an exception to confidentiality. While there are exceptions to confidentiality when a client is presently a danger to themself or others, this does not extend to past incidents of violence. The social worker should directly answer the client's question by clarifying policies regarding confidentiality.

125. **A.** Dialectical behavior therapy (DBT) is an evidence-based treatment for emotion dysregulation associated with borderline personality disorder. DBT includes individual psychotherapy, group skills training, telephone coaching, and therapist participation on a consultation team. The skills training group includes modules covering mindfulness, emotion regulation, interpersonal effectiveness, and distress tolerance.

126. **D.** According to the *NASW Code of Ethics*, social workers should not accept goods or services from clients as compensation. Such bartering arrangements are allowable in very limited circumstances, but create the risk of dual relationships or other boundary crossings and violations. In this case, it is best to plan for termination and referral as long as the client does not pose a danger to himself or others.

127. **D.** Sublimation is an ego defense mechanism in which an individual channels unwanted or unhelpful urges into a more acceptable or productive outlet. In this case, the client's aggressive urges are leading him to get into physical fights, resulting in dangerous situations and potential disciplinary action. By recommending he participate in a martial arts program, the social worker is providing a more acceptable outlet for the client's aggression.

128. **B.** Regression is an ego defense mechanism in which an individual reverts to an earlier developmental stage. In this case, the client is likely experiencing significant stress during finals week, and as a

way of protecting the ego from this stress he has unconsciously regressed to an earlier stage and began wetting the bed.

129. **B.** In this case, the social worker should begin with acknowledging the client's feelings. In the engagement phase of the helping process, social workers must build rapport through a non-judgmental attitude, respect of the client's worth and dignity, and acceptance of the client's right to self-determination. Resistance is normal, but through building rapport the social worker can develop the client's sense of trust.

130. **C.** Encountering clients out in the community is a source of anxiety for many social workers, but it does not have to be a problem. It is best to behave normally, as seeking to avoid a client could draw attention to the potential social worker - client relationship. On the other hand, the social worker should not approach the client, as this would pose risks to confidentiality as well. There is no need for the social worker to leave the situation; this could also create an uncomfortable or awkward situation if it is noticeable.

131. **A.** Secondary prevention refers to strategies intended to reduce further risk or harm among populations that already have a particular illness or injury. Interventions directed toward the general population comprise primary prevention, while in the last answer choice, palliative care refers to tertiary prevention.

132. **A.** Social workers have an obligation to terminate treatment when it is no longer needed. In this case, the client has reported a significant reduction in symptoms and that he is using the skills gained in therapy. No other goals have been identified, and so there is no need for further sessions at this time.

133. **C.** Classroom observation is considered the best way to assess the student's behavior at school. Other assessment methods, such as

a home visit, in-office visit, or parent visit can be useful in gaining a more holistic understanding of the student. However, they would be less helpful in assessing school behavior.

134. **A.** Mary Richmond's concept of a social diagnosis was one of the earliest writings in the field of social casework and a precursor to the later concept of person-in-environment. According to Richmond, poverty and social exclusion could be understood through people's relationship with their social environment.

135. **A.** According to the *NASW Code of Ethics*, social workers should examine and keep current with new knowledge in the field of social work. Social workers are specifically expected to review professional literature and participate in continuing education activities covering both social work practice and professional ethics.

136. **C.** This client has symptoms likely consistent with bipolar disorder, as the case example describes both depressive and manic symptoms. Clients with manic symptoms are typically not prescribed antidepressant medication unless it is combined with a mood stabilizer. Lithium is a commonly prescribed mood stabilizer for clients with bipolar disorder.

137. **C.** The mode is a statistical measure of central tendency, which describes the data point that most frequently appears in the results. This is different from other measures of central tendency such as mean (the average), median (the middle data point), and range (the difference between the highest and lowest data points).

138. **A.** Cultural competence refers to the social worker's ability to navigate cultural differences. As the definition implies, social workers can and do work with clients who have different backgrounds, beliefs, and identities. According to the *NASW Code of Ethics*, social workers should seek out education and develop

an understanding of social diversity and oppression, and should be able to demonstrate knowledge of practice with different cultures.

139. **D.** The situation described in this example is most consistent with the concept of burnout. Social workers experiencing burnout often show signs such as physical and emotional exhaustion, increased irritability, and a feeling of being ineffective in their work. While the social worker could also be experiencing secondary trauma, this would have different signs that are not mentioned in the question.

140. **C.** Increased irritability, being easily startled, and having nightmares are all signs of both post-traumatic stress disorder and of secondary trauma. In this case, the social worker is exposed to extreme levels of stress while caring for patients who are experiencing serious threats to their lives. Secondary traumatic stress is a likely reaction to working in this environment.

141. **A.** There are a number of misconceptions and mixed messages in the field regarding physical touch between a social worker and client. According to the *NASW Code of Ethics*, social workers should not engage in physical contact with clients when there is a possibility of harm to the client. However, the *Code of Ethics* also states that, when social workers do engage in appropriate physical contact with clients, they must set clear, appropriate, and culturally sensitive boundaries.

142. **C.** The action is unethical as the social worker did not obtain client consent. According to the NASW Code of Ethics, social workers should obtain consent before conducting an internet search on the client. The Code of Ethics states that exceptions can be made for protecting the client or others from serious,

imminent, or foreseeable harm, or when there are other compelling reasons for the search.

143. **B.** The social worker's primary responsibility is to the client, not to the employee assistance program. Based on the social worker's assessment, the client requires longer term treatment. Therefore, the social worker should assist the client in obtaining access to longer term treatment. As with all social work interventions, these sessions should be documented as usual.

144. **C.** There are many reasons why clients may wish to reduce their drinking, as the potential negative effects of alcohol use extend beyond those individuals who meet criteria for a DSM-5 alcohol use disorder. The client may not need to eliminate alcohol entirely, and the social worker should respect the client's self-determination. In this case, the social worker should collaborate with the client to set goals and to develop a plan for working toward those goals.

145. **A.** Self-care includes a range of activities to reduce stress and to maintain health and well-being. While there is sometimes a tendency to describe occasional acts of indulgence as self-care, it is important that social workers also have a comprehensive and ongoing plan for self-care. This may include regular exercise, but can also be broader than this.

146. **D.** In operant conditioning, the words positive and negative refer to the addition or subtraction of a stimulus, while reinforcement and punishment refer to efforts to increase or decrease a behavior. In this case, the teacher is taking away (subtracting, i.e., negative) recess time in order to decrease (punish) an undesired behavior.

147. **D.** In Erickson's psychosocial stage of integrity vs. despair, older adults reflect back on their lives and seek to find meaning in their

experiences. They may struggle with the question of how they are leaving a better world for others. In this case, difficulties with this stage are a possible cause of the client's depressed mood.

148. **A.** When a client abruptly changes the subject, it is a likely sign of resistance. Clients often display resistance when they are pushed to change or to explore a topic before they are ready. Resistance can be understood as coming from the interaction between the social worker and the client; thus, the social worker should change their techniques to better align their interventions with the client's goals.

149. **A.** The "miracle question" is a technique drawn from solution-focused therapy. In this technique, the social worker asks the client to imagine a possible world in which their problems no longer exist and their issues have been addressed. In its different forms, this question serves the purpose of leading the client to develop insight and develop their goals for therapy.

150. **D.** Human relations theory provides a model for organizational management in which the psychological needs and relational experiences of workers are the main focus. Developed in response to scientific management theory, human relations theory seeks to help employees feel valued and engaged, ultimately improving the success of the organization.

Jeremy Schwartz, LCSW is a social work educator with extensive clinical practice and teaching experience. A 2011 recipient of the NYU President's Service Award, he has served in teaching roles at New York University and at the Icahn School of Medicine at Mount Sinai, and has provided tutoring to social workers preparing for the Bachelor's, Master's, and Clinical level ASWB examinations. A skilled clinician, he has treated hundreds of patients both in private practice and at The Mount Sinai Hospital, where he served on the Professionalism Committee in the Department of Social Work Services.

www.ingramcontent.com/pod-product-compliance
Lightning Source LLC
Chambersburg PA
CBHW060252030426
42335CB00014B/1666